MW01241658

A Cluster of Acorns

A Collection of Poetry

David Crowell

Published by David A. Crowell
P.O. Box 721817
Oklahoma City, OK 73172 USA

zendt@yahoo.com

Dedication:

To my wife Victoria,
Who has been there with me
through it all.

In Nature

Fall In The Ancient Mountains

I.

Fall in these mountains is not a dramatic affair.
While elk and bison eat their fill of grass
To get through this winter as they have in seasons past
The trees turn straight to brown then suddenly are bare.

Dominant colors are brown and yellow and bronze
For both the grass and on the leaf covered path.
Winter nights soon unleash their freezing wrath
And will only reluctantly warm with dawns.

II.

These mountains provide a place
For bison to have space
And for white-tail deer
To winter another year.

But even in this place
Caution wild turkey
As the sly coyote
Is still here to give chase.

III.

There on the ridge, is that a boulder
or might it be a bison shoulder?
A ton of hide, horn and attitude
preparing for winter's interlude.

On the trail is that water rushing
or leaves the wind are hushing?
Regardless which it is - now
winter will silence stream and bough.

IV

The campground is not silent,
not even very quiet
given the cacophony of cicada and cricket.
There's the occasional elk bugling,
during the annual fall rutting
but the day is not over yet.

As the evening wears on
the insects still drone
and the elk bed down fairly soon.
Things start to get quiet
but soon there's a riot
as coyotes start yipping at the moon.

V.

The cycle of the ages
brings no new stages.
Its all been seen before.
While the earth reposes
the annual cycle closes
then Spring awakes once more.

A Spring-fed Creek

It seems other-worldly to be near
spring water that is so incredibly clear
that a whole ecosystem can be viewed.

There are water bugs with skills imbuded
to walk on water in their search for food.
Patience reveals small fish are in the stream.

Finding them here would certainly make it seem
they needn't worry about predators further downstream.
With their safety here they'll wait and not hurry.

Disturb some rocks and watch how crawfish scurry
leaving dirt suspended in a flurry.
And on the banks fragile flowers bloom.

In the crowded forest here is room
nestled in this creek bed as a womb
for fragile life to prove that it is dear.

A Walk In Winter

When I went out walking this morning,
the temperature was cold.
I go walking every morning,
the sunrise to behold.

The snow flurries I saw were falling,
the grass encrust with ice.
The temperature was also falling;
weather was not so nice.

The air is filled with frozen silence,
with snowflakes drifting down.
Birds are puffed up in their silence
as winter gripped the town.

I think that I will go home now
before I get frostbite.
I'll brew a pot of coffee now,
my house is just in sight.

Sometimes I tire of winter weather
I wish the cold away.
But in the heat of summer weather
I'll think back on this day.

An Oak In Winter

Seeing a luxuriant and ageless oak
with long years of weathering
causes the memory to evoke
times when ice and snow came roaring.

Some winter's mild with little stress,
as weather-wise caterpillars don
appropriate winter weather dress,
predicting temperate skies stay on.

But oft as not the storms descend
and pummel flora with ice and snow.
The weight from both the branches bend
dealing trees a crippling blow.

As the winter storm descends
with its coat of ice and snow,
each heavy laden limb now bends
as the weight brings each one low.

With branches hung like lifeless limbs,
useless with no benefits.
The future is now looking grim,
for loud's the sound when timber splits.

When the storm departs the sky
its time to see what it has wrought.
Damage so bad it makes one sigh
to see destruction that's been brought.

Limbs to ground encrust in ice
with others dangling limp and smashed.
The storms that come exact a price
and leave a land that's fractured and gashed.

An oak with trunk wide as a barrel,
it bears a canopy that's rife
with gaps where birds and squirrels dwell
and find the storm's left all in strife.

With broken branches leaving nubs
the tree is now forced to embrace
among all the other stubs
that storms have left within this space.

But oaks are hardy, long-lived trees
and survive the worst of weather.
Whether heat or winter freeze
it will prosper altogether.

Years from now the damage here
will only be a memory.
The breaks and wounds will disappear
as time provides the remedy.

Through the past it's thrived and fought
ever since the acorn sprout.
Maybe gnarled, maybe not
but skyward it will still reach out.

(continued on next page)

Though storms may come they also go
and what they do is leave behind
a legacy of ebb and flow,
test and honor intertwined.

Clouds

The normal sky in "flyover land"
is total cloud, or no cloud at all.
Be it summer, winter, spring or fall
let grass be short or of full height
skies of blue and puffy white
seldom grace our pasture land.

A full gray sky or total blue
is what one normally muddles through;
but to have white clouds to grace our day
sends cares and ills upon their way.

Day and Night

From where I stand
I'd rather remand
the night unto the day.

The sunrise bright
is such a site,
I'd prefer it here to stay.

But night it seems
has its dreams
that it must convey.

Stars so bright,
such a sight,
blows the day away

with its stars,
and firefly jars
and the Milky Way.

With days so bright
and night just right
It's better left this way.

It Was Just A Day

I. (A Day Hiking)
Today I had a free day to go hiking.
It's always nice to get away
and let your thoughts go their way.
A kind of day much to my liking.

The day was spent above a lake
on trails that gave a splendid view.
I watched the egrets as they flew
I watched the progress of a snake.

I saw a meadow from a distance,
lovely, lush and quite appealing.
Yes, my attention it was stealing
I'll go there next time, perchance.

Clouds were drifting through the skies,
a woodpecker punctuated the day.
Young fawns in the grass would play
and streams were rife with dragonflies.

II. (Evening - campground)
I've waited all day for this moment,
the time when human chatter ends,
the sounds of nature now transcends
the sounds of steel and cement.

It's as though a switch were turned
moving from stage to stage.
Its been the same throughout the age.
Night honors it's nocturne.

III. (Nightfall)
Shadows creep across the land
crows then call to come to roost
as though they need to have excuse
to call out to their cawing band.

Grasshoppers popping their wings in flight,
cicadas heard from miles away.
Ducks and geese across the bay.
Doves announce the start of night.

There's music as the wind blows low
and harmonizes in the trees.
Quite a symphony comes from these
as the moon sets the scene aglow.

IV. (Meditation)
The day I spent was nothing special,
just a quiet day alone,
a day in nature on my own,
a day spent free of show and tell.

As I sit here in the darkness
I reflect upon the day.
Though my youth has gone away
I am blessed, nevertheless.

I ask God grant me quiet evenings
under His cathedral skies.
May I in all things be wise
and seek His peace above all things.

National Park Itinerary

I've climbed the dunes at Great Sand Dunes,
I've photographed White Sands.
I walked amongst the Redwood Trees,
and still have other plans.

I've seen the layered Smokey Mountains,
I've seen the Canyon Grand.
I have marveled at the Landscape Arch,
Such wonders in this land!

A swamp boat in the Everglades
and Carlsbad underground.
Mount Rainier up in the clouds
are beauties I have found.

Petrified Forest and Painted Desert,
Rocky Mount National Park,
Yellowstone and Grand Teton,
even the Gateway Arch.

The Badlands' stripes and the Wind Cave,
I've been to Joshua Tree.
What a stunning view is seen
when in Yosemite.

And for Anasazi ruins
Mesa Verde's unique.
One thousand year-old cliff dwellings,
a culture at its peak.

Theodore Roosevelt National Park,
and Going To The Sun,
seen in Glacier way up north,
impresses every one.

So many places I have seen,
places that I know.
Yet so many still remain,
so many more to go!

Patterns

Leaves are falling,
autumn's coming,
'round again we go.
Shadow lengthens,
darkness strengthens,
winter's soon we know.

Seasons will have their season.
Discourse will have its reason.
Now I find …
never mind,
to break the pattern is treason.

Leaves turn brown and then they fall;
they spiral to the ground.
Just like us, one and all,
we're to the pattern bound.

Reality Check

The rising sun is low on the horizon
as we move from night to a new morning,
silhouetting the tall pine trees
before the day begins its warming.

Rays of light break through the trees and branches
with streams of light that hit the morning mist
rising from the water here before me
that cares not whether I exist.

The Night Birds' Call (Nocturne)

In Oklahoma, which I call home,
oceans are distant but bison roam.
Lakes are blue and pastures green,
wind is free and air is clean.

Though some may laugh and others scorn,
I am of the soil born.
Keep your cities tall and gray
I've no use for their decay.

While cities riot and while cities fall.
I'll listen to the night birds' soothing call.

Two Oaks

I saw an old pair standing stately, proudly in the sun.
Side-by-side with branches tightly, staunchly intertwined.
It was apparent what the ages and the wind had done.
In winter their bareness showed the nests that were left
behind
as generations successfully launched leaving one-by-one.

Soon ready for another season, they put out the green
and serve to anchor the annual renewal of this pastoral scene.

Weather Change

While the morning sun casts my shadow long
the cool, brisk air reminds my heart of song.
I'm alone with my thoughts, where I belong.
I will quietly walk, just gliding along.

The wind rustles the dried leaves
in the upper reaches of the trees.
But weather is coming, nature to please.
We'll soon have more than this gentle breeze.

Oak and Stone, Water and Grass

I sit here in quiet contemplation
gazing on the mirror lake's reflection.
Water so still the clouds and trees
stand silent, frozen in the absence of breeze.

This is a land of rugged duty
where nature displays her aged beauty.
The lake's reflections present contrasts
of oak and stone, water and grass.

Stone from mountains' now rugged stubs
eroded through years to rounded nubs.
Oak imposing in number alone
a cross timbers thicket has plainly grown.

Yes oak and stone, water and grass
will remain as eons pass.
Habitat so diverse this scene
in brown and blue and verdant green.

Just You, Alone

When you walk on a trail another has blazed,
When you follow a route you didn't prepare,
And you failed to negotiate life's maze,
You're not leaving any sign you were there.

If you find you breathe on mirrors
To confirm that there's still life
In a shell now lacking rigors
And with its members causing strife

Then get off the beaten trail,
Take a chance and maybe fail.
Get out of your comfort zone -
Venture out, just you, alone.

A Connection To The Plains

No longer rolling but now drawn fine
the horizon of the plains
greets me with a solid line
that keeps my psyche sane.

There's something of a prairie field
that connects one to the past.
An anchor for the soul revealed
to a land that's vast.

But I go east or I go west,
spirit in disarray,
my heart won't know a calming rest
without the plains this day.

I've seen the mountains and the seas,
I've seen the canyons too,
with tallgrass prairie and gnarled trees -
my spirit will renew.

Life Is A River

Life is a river that flows to the sea;
forever running, forever free.

Starts with a trickle and grows to a creek;
some grow large and others stay meek.

A creek to a stream growing in size;
and a river to stay 'til its demise.

All rivers end as they meet the sea;
for the sea portends eternity.

Some lives are short and others are long
some hurry while others meander along.

Some lives are tragic while others are blest
Some take it serious while others just jest.

Some steps will make and others will break
Some bring joy and others heart ache.

There's no "next time" and no "opt out" -
Experience is what life's all about.

We're there at the start and there at the end;
all seasons of life one must attend.

Life is a river that flows to the sea;
long may it run for you and for me.

Fog At The Trailhead

Fog will dampen every sound,
make things silent all around.
Fog will make the wind stand still
bringing round a moistened chill.

As it softens every sound
it muffles noise from all around.
Room is made for pleasant word
normally silent, never heard:

running water from a brook,
heard from nature's overlook,
the trail then shares a small bird's song,
overlooked when noise is strong.

The crunch of grass beneath one's feet
when hiking boot and dry earth meet
bring to mind an earlier day
before our cares lead us away.

The full, fresh air upon the trail
allows our spirit to unveil
the sense of pleasure that we seek
in a small bird's song and rushing creek.

Birding

I tried my had at birding today
with my new telephoto lens.
It won't focus close, only far away
it's a big telephoto lens.

The only movement that I saw
were hanging leaves now long stale,
there were no birds, no birds at all.
Not one bird I now bewail.

Birds were heard by none were seen,
their distinctive cries and calls.
I heard them all but saw none preen
I have no pictures to enthrall -
I saw no birds at all.

There were no hawks thermal'ing,
no woodpeckers pecking,
no crows crowing,
no robins bobing
and no chickadees chickadeeing.

I guess I'm not a natural birder,
but what could be more absurder
than to see no birds at all?
Looks like I'm not a natural birder,
perhaps I should be a crossworder
since I saw no birds at all.

Well, I ended this day
and got to my car
and finally saw signs of a bird.
I have this much to say
they were generous by far
but their actions were really absurd.

The birds all knew where my car was at
so my windshield was covered by voluminous "splat".
The birds had this day
There's no more to say
They got me - it's just as simple as that.

The American Southwest

Chaco Canyon

Encounter The Canyon

Entering Chaco Canyon is stepping back in time.
It's a place that time forgot,
that became an afterthought,
that was lost and forgotten for a thousand year decline.

At first light, the break of dawn, sunlight streaming
down the canyon, lighting walls
revealing long lost history's halls,
leaving canyon and the ruin walls each gleaming.

Anchoring the canyon at one end is the butte
known as Fajada, the belted one,
Standing bold before the sun
it holds secrets of the canyon most resolute.

Through the eons it has stood, a silent sentinel
watching over all the canyon,
in times of wealth and of abandon
presiding over summer heat and winter chill.

From inside the canyon one finds massive ruins,
great houses, once a source of pride,
filled with ancient works inside
while shear walls conceal the canyon treasures within.

Water's precious in this dry and arid place.
Chaco Wash is the main source
and as it wanders through its course,
it's meager presence the living canyon must embrace.

Surrounding the area are outlier locations and other sites
connecting remote people here.
From the distance they appear,
coming by road for trade and ceremonial rites.

This is Chaco, once a culture grand and vast.
An economic capital
with an influential sprawl;
a place of prominence the centuries have passed.

Fajada Butte

Presiding proudly over the canyon
for ages, ever the faithful companion.
Distinct with ceremonial ramp
and dwelling for a priest to encamp.

In Chaco time is measured by season
and a marker is the reason
to celebrate the passing of time,
following Fajada's demanding climb.

The Sun Dagger marks the passing
of seasons by piercing the coiling
by the sun of the petroglyph
concealed above the butte's sheer cliff.

An unknown ceremony greets
the sun as Chaco now entreats
a prosperous season just ahead
based on how the sky was read.

Roads

Ceremony and ritual
need a place to be observed.
Progressing toward a spiritual
site, the road proceeds uncurved.

Boulevard style roads it seems
serve for transport and as shrine.
Used to gather building beams
and processional in line.

Thirty feet wide and arrow straight,
roads proceed by ladder and stair
over cliff as terrain dictates,
a dedicated thoroughfare.

Astro-archaeology

Construction of buildings based upon
cardinal direction and solar alignment
give special meaning to the canyon
and honor the sun's rising glint.

It's a thousand years ago
and as the sun is rising
the watchers of the sun arise
to begin their daily consulting.

The duty is theirs to watch the seasons
and declare the sun's advance.
Over years they've tracked it's path
across the sky's immense expanse.

Signaling spring and planting time
from many observation sites,
the gazers were able to define
seasons changes from sky lights.

This was a people with surprising skill
at charting movements of the sky.
No written language but yet still
the sky was theirs to codify.

Great Houses

At the center of Chaco culture
are the Great Houses of the canyon.
They appear much like a mansion
but are vital infrastructure.

Walls of stone with rubble core
reaching four to five stories,
floor joists made from distant pine trees
and greasewood cross planks for the floor.

Built with kivas for ceremony
and plazas for large gatherings,
they serve as centers meant for trading
like turquoise and rare abalone.

Treasures of the Chacoans
were turquoise, cacao and macaws.
The riches here would give one pause,
all things that came from other lands.

In the way they are designed,
the layout of the building is key.
A Great House must appear as stately
and each astronomically aligned.

In each House are hundreds of rooms,
walls are covered with mortar and clay,
sheltered from weather with small doorways,
and rooms sealed off for ancient tombs.

Few rooms made with hearth or window;
apparently used for storage alone.
Few for habitation known
due to lack of light and airflow.

Conclusion

Chaco's a place that's filled with quiet
and has been for many years.
But a thousand years ago
it was a place of fear and tears.

It's thought the rulers of this place,
were total masters of their sphere,
overseeing massive projects
with labor summoned from far and near.

The Great Houses at Chaco served
as residence for rulers and priests,
dutifully checking every day
the sunrises in the east.

The Sun Dagger had marked the seasons
for those same one thousand years.
It's broken now and not in service,
the dagger itself no longer appears.

The Ancient ones have since deserted
this dry and unforgiving land.
It's now a place where raven soar
and the Houses lie unmanned.

When the sun sets in this place
at the end of every day,
the canyon's one day closer to
the way it started through decay.

Man-made Houses cede their place
of power to the force of time.
Ruins fall to rubble piles
as they succumb to decline.

The elk and coyotes will lay claim
to this land of theirs again,
once it's all returned to earth
and man's presence lie in ruin.

As it was so it will be -
reunited with its past.
The wind and sun will surely reclaim
this arid land again at last.

Other Chaco Thoughts

I.

The supernova pictograph,
a Crab Nebula representation,
painted in display of craft
and not just as a decoration.

II.

Historically known as Anasazi,
the people here now have dispersed.
Navajo for "ancient enemy",
a new name is now rehearsed.

The name preferred to show them honor:
Ancestral Puebloans.
We call them *enemy* no longer,
as Earth continues through its motions.

In The Sacramento Mountains Of New Mexico

Mountain ranges in the southwest
Erode from wind and rain.
They have a tiered or terraced look
Like a brides' cake gone insane.

Tier on tier they rise skyward .
But the bride's not satisfied
Until the limits of its construction
Set rules of reason aside.

On each tier is rubble strewn
From erosion just above
And over time its fit to grow
The southwest flora thereof.

But seldom is an access route
From one tier to the next.
So here we have a beautiful site
Who's access leaves me vexed.

Bands of beige reveal the stone
With green the trim below.
A lovely spot up in the sky
Footstep will never know.

An Island In The Sky

I.

A butte is an island in the sky
less wide than it is high.
While a mesa has a wider scale
yet similar in most detail.

II.

Where caprock covers a weaker earth layer
erosion will take the easier route.
But since the caprock's strength is greater
the softer material will first wash out.

Over time as earth gives way
the caprock covered part remains.
The results of this we see today
As mesas and buttes amongst the plains.

III.

The caprock layer
is a vertical barrier
straight up from rubble
sloughed off in tumble
over eons of time
leaving a climb
to get to the top
of this outcrop.

IV.
From the top one sees hawks
and vultures on the thermals.
Eating their catch on rocks
while others continue their circles.

Amidst fowl hunters
butte residents cower
behind rock, bush and tree.
Lest one blunders
and a hunter devour
prey found among butte debris.

V.
Life on top of a butte
is primarily insect and bird;
birds in constant dispute
with singing by man unheard.

From atop is a view
seen but by few;
a view that's seldom seen,
because assent to the crest
is anything but routine
and quite a physical test.

(Continued on next page)

VI.

I found a butte with assisted access
that allowed me to climb to the heights.
With ladder in place
I climbed to embrace
this lofty, restricted showplace.
And now I find I must confess
how beautiful were the views and the sights.

VII.

Once on the top I stopped to take in
the quiet afforded by this place.
Hearing only the wind I began herein
to breathe deeply with a feeling of grace.

Calm and peace, and tranquility
await you when you disconnect
from the parking lot filled with liability.
This is the perfect time to reflect.

VIII.

There's much we can learn
if we willingly discern
the rhythm and peace of this place.
If we only slow down,
get outside of town
and cut back our unnatural pace.

Wichita Mountains

Time is a great equalizer
for mountains grand in scale
find they are no more than overture
to the main acts' eroding tale.

Granite spires giving way
to freeze and thaw and wind and rain
leave piles of granite blocks that say
"In spite of this we will remain".

And remain they do in silence still
watching 'or as ages pass
while boulders crumble and valleys fill
and rubble's overrun with grass.

What fate befalls these massive blocks?
What destiny awaits this jumbled lot?
"Time" advises that these rocks
will still be here when you are not.

So care not for the fate of spires
nor of mountains God has wrought.
Their erosion never tires
but they'll still be here when you are not.

Fall In The Ancient Mountains

I.
Fall in these mountains is not a dramatic affair.
While elk and bison eat their fill of grass
to get through this winter as they have in seasons past
the trees turn straight to brown then suddenly are bare.

Dominant colors are brown and yellow and bronze
for both the grass and on the leaf covered path.
Winter nights soon unleash their freezing wrath
and will only reluctantly warm with dawns.

II.
These mountains provide a place
for bison to have space
and for white-tail deer
to winter another year.

But even in this place,
caution wild turkey
as the sly coyote
is still here to give chase.

III.
There on the ridge, is that a boulder
or might it be a bison shoulder?
A ton of hide, horn and attitude
preparing for winter's interlude.

On the trail is that water rushing
or leaves the wind are hushing?
Regardless which it is - now
winter will silence stream and bough.

IV.

The campground is not silent,
not even very quiet
given the cacophony of cicada and cricket.
There's the occasional elk bugling,
during the annual fall rutting
but the day is not over yet.
As the evening wears on
the insects still drone
and the elk bed down fairly soon.
Things start to get quiet
but soon there's a riot
as coyotes start yipping at the moon.

V.

The cycle of the ages
brings no new stages,
it's all been seen before.
While the earth reposes
the annual cycle closes
then Spring awakes once more.

On Government Land

I.

I find myself on Government land
where it's quitting time and the gates get closed.
For a time the park's exposed
to silence as all cars are banned
and the entrance now is barred, unmanned.

II.

The shadows are long as the park seeks refuge in night
for dark conceals the attractions of this site;
the elements that draw the nature seeking crowd
to share this place with beauty endowed
when day is bright and the land is bathed in light.

III.

For a time the land is as it was
adhering only to nature's laws,
of beak and tooth and fang and claws.

IV.

There are many reasons for the crowds to come:
To see red dogs* and full grown bison,
and maybe sun dogs** on the horizon.
Or rather than to be outdone
they hike a trail to get their fun.

Beauty and adventure draw the crowds
who get as up close as they're allowed.
Oft forgetting the place is wild
without restraints for man and child.
Nature will be wild, unbowed.

V.
Regardless your mindset on adventurous whims
Where the pavement ends is where life begins.

VI.
In the morning the gates will open again
but only after a night of rain
which highlights the webs spiders spun
overnight without the sun.
The night is gone but the webs remain.

And that same rain and that same sun
leave brilliant diamonds on the run
for those who look where webs are spun.

*(red dog – new born bison)
** (sun dog – An atmospheric phenomena)

Antelope Canyon Triptych

Entering Antelope Canyon

Looking across the expanse of slick rock
to the horizon blue and tan
there's a crack in the earth of lengthy span
concealed to all except the hawk.

Water is an honored guest
in this hidden sandstone world
for it has formed the curiously curled
features below the sandstone crest.

Water rare and water blest
disturbs the canyons normal rest.
It rushes through in torrent stream
carving sand into a dream.

Yes, slick rock hides what eye can't find
unless one's standing right beside
where rock and wind and rain collide
to carve the crevice nature's mined.

In some spots cathedral walls
appear to rise in silent praise
to the creator of these hallowed ways:
the driving wind and fierce rainfall.

In The Depths

The Sun above casts down its gaze
from miles and miles above.
Shining down its glowing rays
into the depths thereof.

And as the light descends the depth
illuminating our way
we stand spellbound holding our breath
with nothing now to say.

Bands of color brown and gold
orange and of yellow.
Line the path we now behold
in layers as they flow.

And rays of light pick up the dust
that once lay on the floor.
A breath of air, a modest gust
hath brought a specter fore.

Tales it has of times now gone
when it had this place alone.
Before the hoards that come at dawn
when the place was all its own.

We sometimes love a thing to death
and smother it with care
but sometimes nature needs a breath
and guests to go elsewhere.

Sandstone's Beauty

A hundred feet deep and five feet wide,
but varying greatly from side to side;
the canyon snakes its way through rock
that once was solid as a block.

And through this passageway now here
are layers of rock, tier on tier.
Stripes and bands and furls unfold
in patterns heretofore untold.

Each layer has a hue its own,
colors in a wall of stone.
Shades from eons long ago
through the age's ebb and flow.

These subtle hues each state their case
why they're most lovely in this place.
But each and everyone's undone
'less it's lit up by the sun.

The Sun reflects from wall to wall,
sending light into this hall,
illuminating every band
in this canyon made of sand.

Hidden from the world we see
in this land of rock and scree
is beauty in another realm,
beauty that will overwhelm.

Modern Life

A Decision

I'm trudging forward with my head down,
leaning into the wind.
The path ahead is ominous,
with trials around each bend.

Had I but known the uncertainty
of my chosen route
I would have had more second thoughts,
of that there is no doubt.

For better or worse the die is cast,
my course is firmly laid.
My inner fears will now concede
the piper must be paid.

A Lifetime of Memories

A lifetime of memories took but a moment it seems.
It comprises a life of living and dreaming of dreams.
The way we think and the things we say and do
hearken back to experiences we have been through.

Some of those are things we'd like to share
but some are things only we ourselves should bear.
Whether we like it or not that's the way things are
as we look back on our past, from afar.

And They Kept On Rowing

Time with his grandfather was a cherished treat;
they'd head for the lake in a double heartbeat,
fishing the shoreline in a rusty old boat.
But he grew up, leaving an empty seat,
now it's grandfather alone with his fishing coat
… and he keeps on rowing.

She caught his eye and he caught hers.
They disappointed the restaurateurs
by dating on row boats on Central Park Lake.
It's funny how themes in life recur,
leaving crumbs for ducks in their wake
… and they kept on rowing.

On the job he did his work,
long days and effort he'd never shirk.
The team pulled hard and made progress.
Through his effort he made his mark,
promoted soon for his success
… and the team kept on rowing.

Now in charge and in his prime
he continued up his corporate climb.
But as time is want to do
year on year obliged down time.
So then he bid the team adieu
… and the team kept on rowing.

He finds he's in retirement,
engaged within his final stint.
Time alone with his own boat,
fishing now without a hint
his former life lies so remote
… and he keeps on rowing.

Alternate endings:
(1)
Then at the Styx he is aware
of the boatman waiting there.
"Sir, if you share your destination,
"I bear two coins here for the fare."
But passage was silent through its duration
… and Charon kept on rowing.

(2)
Then at the Jordan he is aware
of the boatman waiting there.
"Will you tell your destination,
"will you Sir our direction share?"
But passage was silent through its duration
… and Michael started rowing.

A Covid-19 Pause

I should be hiking a trail someplace
or engaged in a 5K race.
But I'm stuck here in this neighborhood
while future plans remain obscured.

Covid-19 is running rampant.
What we need is a knight-errant
on his steed and with a cure,
something the virus can't endure.

It's time has come and it will go,
but when for sure we cannot know.
But go it will and 'twill be gone
and normal life will then go on.

Two Friends

Two good friends I lost this year.
in spite of efforts to interfere.
Why 'twas them remains unclear
Who knew the veil to be so shear?

One died of double-hit lymphoma
with family surrounding him.
The other died of Covid-19,
intubated, lone and grim.

One lost life with those well known
and one unseen who died alone.

Both of them will be embraced
when they see Jesus face-to-face.
Faithful followers where they,
who never failed to serve or pray.

Memories forever clear,
two good friends I lost this year.

Thoughts on Job

I.

Like a stillborn child
that never gasps for that first breath
is a newborn child
on the inexorable road to death.

I was there at my first breath
I'll be there at my last
except now for each breath
each hour would be my last.

II.

Your life and mine
are merely crumbs on the plate
in the span of time
on which this world must wait.

But this I know
as the sun shines in the sky
life is but a shadow
and the valley of bones is dry.

Yet the flesh
that once covered those bones
can make fresh
and sharpen a life it hones.

III.

I'll grab today -
embrace this life we share.
And never say
I despair – I do not care.

You Can't Be Too Careful (Vultures)

I saw five vultures circling, circling overhead.
No doubt something's dying, dead or has bled.
I checked my pulse and it was beating, clearly
I'm not dead.
I guess their meal was served up somewhere else instead.

They're like politicians coveting our bread.
"Public good" they cry causing us to dread.
But here's something about vultures, of vultures
I have read:
you can't be too careful till all are dead or fed.

Death Is Hard

Dying is always a hard affair.
Left behind are those who love and care
Calendars full with tasks undone:
Furniture to refinish, miles to be run,
Grandkids to hug and lessons to give.
The forge lies silent, the knives undone.
The craftman's missing - life's a sieve.

Dying is always a hard affair.
Leaving behind those we love in despair.
But the moment has now flown.
My life cut short leaves panic full-blown.
But while you scurry, morn and fret
My existence continues yet.

I've moved onto another plane
From a life I'll never gain again.
Carry on as best you can
I have pressing matters at hand
That supersede your temporal span.

Thank you for your caring
In the life that we were sharing.
Thank you so much
For your tender touch.
But its best we move on
With the new dawn.

Please don't forget me
But its time to let me … go.

Lonely Proximity

I.

The morning sun shines through a window
finding married strangers in a bed
who now regret the day they wed.

With hearts now separated by shadow
lying there in icy distance
experiencing legal coexistence.

II

Long lost are the memories of a Jamaican beach,
hands no longer extend to reach
the one once loved but now denying
that rebuilding is worth trying.

III.

Once there was a halo,
now its broken though.
The words have become cruel
and every day a duel.

Solo is a lonely way to be
and at times one cannot see
a way beyond lonely proximity,
when love's returned so dismally.

IV.
Nursing a drink at a bar
on a solo business trip
that takes one away, afar
with respite from brinkmanship
knowing there's no love waiting at home,
a world of color, now monochrome.

V.
The pain is strikingly real
as a heart tries to heal
but its a long, sad road
to lose this loathsome load.

But as the sun rises
midst tomorrow's surprises
he'll look past the dread
to a new day ahead.

Middle of the Night

Sometimes my past comes calling in the middle
of the night.
I confess it's a pretty unpleasant sight.

I've been over the mountains of the moon
so all that's left is the valley of the shadow,
but that's a pretty lonely trip *
that I'm not excited to start soon.
It's a trip I have to take though
but its one I'd rather skip.

You are not wrong who deem
that my days have been a dream. **
As one who's road was laid out
Not knowing what's life's about
Going from point A to point B,
Be it here or across the sea,
Doing each expected task
Without ever stopping to ask
"Is this really what I want to do?
"You know we are depending on you."
Take this kiss upon the brow
And in parting from you now... **
The road taken seemed preordained
With my agreement unrestrained.
Sometimes life gets in the way
Of other options for the day.
Is all that we see or seem
But a dream within a dream? **

Regrets:
Regrets are there by the score
And they don't start with the music store.
Years before that little hand
Should've made a fist, took a stand.
It's okay, my tears dried with time
Except for regret over nickel and dime.

Is anyone here?
Does anyone hear?
Feels like I'm in a well
A few feet short of Hell.

Caught up in the turnstile of life
Circling round from strife to strife
More care for me than for my wife.

I was a child and she was a child
In this kingdom by the sea. ***
My mind runs wild as regrets are piled -
But the blame remains with me.

Assessment:
I'm not who I was; I'm not who I want to be;
I'm not yet who I will be.
But I must get past my past
Before the future is forever cast.
Thus much let me avow... **
I must be who I want to be now.

(Continued on next page)

Confession:
I used to hope someone would take my hand
As I walk into that Night.
But now these days I understand
I live by faith and not by sight.

Our "Great Hope" has been my song
But I won't know for sure till I die
So if it turns out that I was wrong
I'll never know it was all a lie.

What a waste it would be if death is, in fact, the end.
If there were no call for my soul to ascend.

But the things I've done through the faith
Were not done for reward.
Disaster relief must be forthwith
To make someone else's life less hard -
To show Christ's love with no-holds-barred.

So much learned and so much gained
One's "Hope" must be sincere, unfeigned. ****

Final Instructions:
no, no, no don't bury me,
don't put me in that cold, cold clay
burn me with refiner's fire
hot, to burn the dross away.

And should I stand, or kneel,
before our God some day
No doubt speechless, unable to say
The gratitude I'd feel
That
This life of mine so filled with flaw
Would place me before Him, in awe.

References:
*Eldrado
** A Dream Within A Dream
*** Annabel Lee
**** Titus 2:13

Thoughts On Equality

A hotly debated subject
And one you might expect
from a people undergoing change
from a people foregoing change.

Given one's circumstances
what are the chances
to have equality?
Can we even speak
in honest critique
of it with civility?

You and I are different
but it is inherently apparent
we both have basic rights
which should not be basis for fights.

Our access should be equal
Our protection should be equal
Our opportunity should be equal.
And let us not forget about this business
of life, liberty and pursuit of happiness.

These should all be in place
but if not, its a disgrace.

Not one of us starts better than some
nor worse than others.
But some may have had it worse with
fathers and mothers.

Two start equal but one is honed
and the sequel – one is bemoaned.
A seed may be carefully cultivated
or it could be neglected.
What I've just stated may be outdated
but neglect leaves one ill fated
and negatively effected.

Or, perish the thought,
what if life wrought
someone with high level abilities?
Abilities highly sought
to which no level of thought
could have forged these capabilities.

Regardless the hand that one's been dealt,
Its there where one's life is dwelt.
So live life and blame refuse
Don't live a life of constant excuse.

Naked I came into this world and naked I will leave it.
I may not be as talented as some
But when it's my time to succumb
What I've made of it was up to me – every bit.

Love, Romance and Family

Christmas 2020

Snow is falling near, my love.
There's snow upon the ground.
Snow is falling from above,
its blanket leaves no sound.

It's Christmas now and without doubt,
you have my heart my dear.
My love you'll find to be devout,
you'll find it ever near.

So as the snow bestills the Earth,
and brings it to a calm,
your love for me has given birth
to peace as from a Psalm.

In my heart my constant prayer
is that in Heav'n you'll say
he may have loved me without flair
but he loved me all the way.

The Love We Share

The love we share has stood the test
which others could not do.
For through it all, despite the rest,
my love is just for you.

So when we fight and say those things
which should be left unsaid,
just know that love will always bring
my best for you instead.

And when we meet on distant shores
midst stars in life above,
I hope you'll know that I adored
you as my only love.

Yes, There is Love

While looking at you smiling,
I see you quite beguiling.
My photos now remind me,
Of our love's beginning.
To my heart you have the key.

The lock was once closed tight, dear.
Traveling in my own sphere,
You altered my conclusion,
I know your love's sincere.
You are love's confirmation.

Husbands and Wives

In much the way a couple's photograph
shows images of two lives,
a photograph can never show
the interdependence of husbands and wives.

Years ago with vows we pledged our love
with hand in hand and hearts wide open.
And somehow two lives were merged in a way
that I could not have imagined then.

It's been many years, may it be many more, that we
spend meeting the needs of each other.
And with my hand in yours and your hand in mine,
we'll walk through each new day together.

Mother's Day 2020

I can't imagine going through this life
without us being side by side.
Thank you for being my loving wife,
our sons' mother, my darling bride.

Many years have passed since our "I Do's"
but "love's" a word I still claim and use.
My feelings for you without doubt.
are what lifelong love is all about.

An Old Man's Hands

There was once an old man in my life.
While differences between us were rife
there probably was more in common
than not between me and this old man.

Some might call him "The Old Man"
but I only did that once and he began
to deliver a lecture on the disrespect
the title bore, every aspect.

I expect in times now past
he'd used the title unabashed.
The lesson he learned at his dad's hand,
likely more severe than my reprimand.

But then again, knowing my dad
and knowing he was not a compliant lad -
he'd probably used the forbidden phrase
to make his father's ire blaze.

While there was much we did not share,
agreement on politics was rare,
as well as religion and with music.
I dare not challenge his touch with a cue stick.

We did, however, share one trait,
It wasn't stride or walking gait
but, rather, it was our hands.
Just genetic, nothing planned.

His were the hands of a workman
Who's disdain of pretense was certain.
Hands meant for heavy equipment,
Lava soap and honest commitment.

There's more about him I could tell
and memories of him still with me dwell
but I've found the core of a man
is in the heart more than the hand.

You Are A Blessing
(To A Niece)

At the start of every morning until the fall of night,
there are very special people who always take delight
in helping meet the needs of others by being a
shining light.

No "thanks" or "bless you" is necessary nor is
even sought,
just the chance to help another is the lesson taught,
standing straight in confidence, never seen distraught.

And this is how I see you, be it right or wrong.
Meeting needs of others, in your voice a song.
In the hearts of many you always will belong.

Of My Sons

My sons have hit the ground running,
or so the saying goes.
Each has had their share of joys
but each their share of woes.

I wish I could have them back again,
each as a little boy.
For with perfect future knowledge,
I'd probably change my tact
to better prepare them for life ahead
and then to redeploy.
Many things I taught them I'm
sure I would retract
in favor of many lessons I
learned the hard way -
to wave them off from many things
meant to lead astray.

Not that I would want my history
placed upon their lives -
just to see them better prepared
for troubles that arise.

To My Sons

I'm not expecting perfection, no father ever will be.
Just hoping you will be a better father than me.

And gratefully after these few years of watching you
with your own children I am now confident
that in your lives there is always a sure intent
to have the best of being a good parent come through.

Putting self aside as well as pride
a selfless nature is exemplified
as you take your families to your side
and put them first with ego denied.

Fragments

Tiny yellow flowers,
so hard to photograph.
A breeze will make them giggle -
the wind will make them laugh.

-*-

The old gravel road got a new layer of rock
ground from a hill of quartz -
it looked like diamonds on my walk,
like jewels from English courts.

-*-

I heard the sound of thunder,
'twas comforting to hear
It means the lightening missed
and I was in the clear.

-*-

Campgrounds now are so much different
than they were "back in the day".
Instead of tents and blazing fires
we've Christmas lights and RV gourmet.

-*-

When you come across a place
whose rhythm meets your pace
it's something to embrace
for you've found your place of grace.

-*-

When I was younger and a runner
the thing I used to say
was
"The wind and the hills never give back
all that they take away."

-*-

Sometimes poetry observes
and sometimes it preaches.
But sometimes it just soaks up sun on sandy beaches.

-*-

Who knows what tomorrow holds?
Certainly not me.
I'll only know as it unfolds,
and then just by degree.
The future's secrets it withholds.
and I don't have the key.

-*-

When you're in a rut
you don't have to steer anymore.
But you'll only go
where someone else has been before.

-*-

When you commit to a husband or to a wife
there's much that forever changes in your life.
There's love for each other in good times and bad
and a warm tender touch when hearts are sad.

-*-

Sometimes poems written at night
are not so good by morning light.

-*-

Long before I knew the art of verse and poetry,
there were writers penning verse I'd know eventually.

-*-

So when it comes to dying
you're out there on your own.
It's too late to keep trying,
you reap what you have sown.

-*-

I'm pretty happy with my life.
I have great sons and a charming wife.
I survived the workplace wars
and retired to lawn and chores.

-*-

Heavy laden clouds of snow,
winds pick up, watch it blow.
There's a blizzard in the forecast,
looks like winter's here at last.

-*-

Walking further down the sidewalk
I saw there laying a dead mouse.
Apparently it was dropped by a hawk.
What a sad day for each house.

-*-

I took a walk in the cool morning,
properly attired.
I came home later,
properly tired.

-*-

I saw a half moon in the sky
midst the white clouds and calming blue.
And as the white clouds scurried by,
the blue remained forever true.

-*-

I walk in quiet solitude on trails that life has blazed.
I stand here in the shadows, looking back amazed.
Many places, many times, many situations
leave me here with questions and --- expectations.

-*-

I had a bout with cancer,
I've gone a round with hell.
I've finished the full treatment
I've rung recovery's bell.

-*-

Faith

In A Cathedral

There is something about a cathedral that ministers to me.
It's grand and cavernous space glories the Almighty.

The heavy oaken doors open to the vestibule,
the place we first meet God, seeking Him and His rule.

The soaring vaulted nave shows the glory of His grace.
The singing from the choir echoes the angels in their place

The transept marks the heart of this hallowed space.
One bends the knee with humble heart, His mercy to
embrace.

Then listen to the tower bells' call to piety.
Peeling out their faithful call to honor Calvary,

The arch'ed windows hearken back to biblical accounts.
The stained glass that they hold's enshrined in generous
amounts.

And Evensong reverberates there in the stony silence.
The music closes out the day in harmony and balance.

I calm my heart, I bend my knee, I bow my head in prayer
Then I listen for His voice with reverence in the air.

I listen for his Still Small Voice and seek His presence
there.
And while I hear it in this place, it could be anywhere.

Anywhere His love is found, anywhere at all.
He calls us all unto Himself, where ere our foot may fall

Cancer and Faith

The diagnosis now is in
my treatment plan must soon begin.
Prognosis seems to offer hope
that a cure may be in scope.
While live I may, or die I might
I will offer up a fight.

But either way it comes to this
the fear I bear I can't dismiss;
if bear I must I'm not alone
for there's a God upon the throne
who walks beside me in the way
and gives me grace to claim each day.

I've practiced faith for many years;
we'll see if Heaven now all cheers
and finds I have embraced my walk
and that my walk has matched my talk.

May I walk the path I face
with confidence and holy grace
and accept what God's ordained
with garments white and life unstained.

Personal Psalms

A Psalm of: Grace

Without power, without strength
I come into your presence.
Without standing but at length
with grace as recompense.

I cannot earn what You give freely,
your grace for my account.
My salvation you decree,
as love flows from your fount.

I am here with gratitude
for what you gladly share.
But grace on earth is only prelude
of Your eternal, loving care.

You give me power to believe,
you are my total source.
Into my soul I know you weave
the strength to stay the course.

A Psalm of: Mercy

I have fallen short again;
I have failed to persevere.
To the Law I don't adhere,
I'm shunning You, embracing stain.

I have your word to show the way,
and your Spirit here to lead,
but in action and in deed
I often choose to roam and stray.

But You show mercy when I sin
and hold back judgment I deserve.
While my heart knows You observe
the ugliness I have within.

You show compassion when I fail
and bring repentance to my heart
for only then do I depart
my error, and your power avail.

Nothing in me warrants mercy,
but it's all I have to plead.
The one thing that I know I need:
"Mercy!" is my humble plea.

A Psalm of: Creation

You, oh Lord, are the creator,
creator, designer and life sustainer
Creator of all that now has life,
author of harmony, not strife.

Glory is yours for who You are,
from Bethlehem's announcement star,
to teaching previously unheard
and to Golgotha's final word.

"Into Thy hands I commend my spirit".
Spoken such that few could hear it
but rocks were rent, the veil was torn
a new paradigm was born.

From the tomb creation found
that it's risen King was crowned.
His creation now reclaimed,
"Hosanna" all the Earth proclaimed.

A Psalm of: Faith and Hope

My faith is a decision and a heart-felt trust in God.
'Tis a faith as tangible as Aaron's budding rod.
I offer up my faith in You afresh each dawning day,
but in that faith I oft have doubts and fear upon me weighs.
To accompany my faith and see me on the way
comes hope designed to strengthen faith and all my fears allay.

The things in which my faith now trusts are evident in hope
for hope embraces unseen things allowing me to cope.
It is hope within our lives allowing us to see
beyond the ridge and trust in things destined yet to be.
But seen or not through hope we grasp ahold of things to come
and though doubt endanger hope, it never will succumb.

The product of my faith is hope for hope is based on faith.
For promises within your Word are based on what Thou saith.
No surer source of faith than this for You have spoken hence:
"You have been given life anew, all at My expense."

A Psalm of: Praise

Alleluia, Praise the Lord!
Exult the one who's most adored.
Lift his name above the rest.
It is Him who's highly blest.

Sing to Him of His great deeds;
sing of how His teaching leads.
Dance within His loving presence,
rejoicing in His holy essence.

In praise we follow his commands,
with instruments and holy hands.
In communion side by side,
we honor Him for how He died.

Most praise though for how he rose,
Him all Hell sought to oppose.
Victory was His alone
as He ascended to His throne.

A Psalm of: Repentance

I come humbly before you my God
with repentance for a life most flawed.
Glory, laud and honor are Yours alone
for it is only you who my sins atone.

In old age I look back on my sins,
from my youth where all of this begins,
through the decades filled with my own pleasure
to this day, they are number without measure.

I have been presumptuous my Lord.
Dismissing my sin lightly inward
but You see what's truly in my heart,
the darkness that has been there from the start.

I can glibly ask you to forgive
the depravity in which I live
but by doing this I plainly reveal
the self-sufficiency I really feel.

So with honest contrition in my heart,
I morn how sin has kept us far apart.
I embrace your love and turn aside
from this life that's filled with sin and pride.

Oh mighty God, Sovereign Ruler of all,
in my darkness now on you I call.
Reach out to me as only You can do
and grant to me a life reborn and new.

Miscellaneous Subjects

Guillotine

To the Guillotine brought
my heart racing
and blood coursing
with palms sweating
mind full of thought.

And then … not.

Guillotine II

I hear the blade a comin'
It's plunging down the slide
My rambling days have ended
In moments I'll have died.
I'm bound here in this gibbet
And time keeps rushing on.
I'm up here on exhibit
I'll soon be dead and gone.

They say it's twenty seconds
your brain keeps functioning,
then The Reaper beckons,
no longer can you cling
to life as you once knew it,
its time this life to quit.
You'll fit now in that casket,
its time this life to quit.

(To the tune of Folsom Prison Blues).

I Wrote A Poem For Myself

I wrote a poem for myself
to see if I could still write rhyme.
I've other things I might've done
like to go out for a run
but since in sport I'm past my prime,
those skills I've put upon the shelf.

So that leaves me much more time
to think and write and craft my rhyme.

Manage Time

Time is going by so fast,
I need a way to make it last.
Soon the present will be the past;
the world is going way too fast.

This is just a little rhyme
about the fleeting fact of time.
Not a nickle or a dime
just a fleeting sense of time.

Fifteen cents won't buy a lot,
once a soda or a pop,
but little things have often taught
that there are things which can't be bought.

Time is something I have learned,
which once spent is not returned.
The time we're given is unearned
but we use it unconcerned
and with objections overturned.

Yesterday feels far away
but does craving it betray
the importance of today?
Or does it merely mean delay
in dealing with the day today?

Embrace the day and don't postpone
subtle things or things well known;
we can not buy back time that's flown,
the use of which is ours to own.
For time well used or time I've blown,
I am responsible alone

The Farmhouse

The farmhouse sets upon a ridge
above a field where cattle grazed.
It serves now as our only bridge
to a time and place where kin were raised.

Father, mother, brothers, sisters
called the little house their home.
On quiet nights the wind still whispers
of lives now only marked by stone.

The screen door slammed when kids raced through
pulled back in place by a worn out spring.
Farm raised kids are quite a crew
who make the fields and valleys ring.

The screened back porch was key to living
for it housed the cistern well.
The pump that always needed priming
and where you bid your guests farewell.

Not to forget the communal dipper
or the enamel water basin,
slop pail for remains of dinner
and the jars all made by "Mason".

In the house activity centered
around the kitchen and front room.
The kitchen stove was where you scented
pecan rolls to chase the gloom.

The front room had the other stove,
the only other source of heat.
In it they'd the firewood shove
in their attempt the cold to beat.

Winters in this drafty house
required blankets by the pile.
And as the eyes would yield to drowse
they'd quilt themselves in patchwork style.

As the stove turned red with heat,
the crank phone on the wall forgotten,
the wooden rockers kept their beat
tomorrow all would start again.

Farm life in these early days
was hard for all concerned.
But in the memory pleasure stays
For family ties so selflessly earned.

Thoughts On Writing

I really do not know
where a poem is going to go
when I start writing it.

The words just seem to flow
as if they want to show
it's them who wrote the writ.

I rebel at that thought
for without me they'd not
have insights to apply.

For words without thought
a poem have never wrought.
Without me they're just a passerby.

Old Boots

It's hard to get rid of old hiking boots
that have seen better days.
However, their usefulness is not over,
just in a new phase.
Now they're used to knock around in
and to mow the lawn.
They've seen their last hiking trip,
seen their last lakeside dawn.

Time In The Land Of The Dead

A dread place where men unwillingly tread.
Quiet's bespread over this land of the dead.

The sun sets slowly leaving view.
For those now here, they have no need;
who at this point will gladly cede
that, as with life, this day is through.

Mausoleum, tomb and stone
all stand silent, but not alone.
In this quiet, darkening place
bodies now the grave embrace.

As for me do nothing rash
but let this body end as ash
and spread throughout the desert wide
with only sagebrush by my side.

No need for space
in this place.
Simply open sky
to occupy.

Fighting Cancer

The Unexpected Guest

1)

It is very melodramatic
and every response is automatic.
"That's so sad, I'm sorry"
"It'll be okay, don't worry."

Nevertheless ...
I go into the unknown,
a path I negotiate alone.
Family and friends are there
but the burden is mine to bear.
They will help the best they can
but ultimately it's my lifespan.
Life seems short and all too brisk
when it's you whose life's at risk.

2)

Though these are here with me
I am the sole invitee
to this date with destiny.

3)

The doctor says she thinks its cancer
but diagnosis hasn't yet an answer.
A scan comes first and then biopsy,
but hopefully it's cancer-free.

Nothing focuses one's thought
as when a person's world is fraught
with cancer as potentially
an option for your malady.

Awaiting Test Results

Still awaiting the biopsy test result
as the lab reviews and the doctors consult.
I'm surprisingly feeling better
as my curiosity grows whetter
to learn what the test results show
and whether I have treatment to undergo.

My throat no longer feels a knife
is there to threaten me my life
when I swallow a meal or a drink.
I don't know what to say or think
as to the reason for this change
but swallowing easy seems so strange.

Surely now in a day or two
results of the test will come through.
Until then I'll anticipate
various scenarios of my fate.

(I'm told biopsies sometimes cause the body to partially
heal but are not a treatment and the gain is temporary.)

Test Results

The day has come to get the diagnosis.
Anxious about the test result,
with the doctor I consult.
In somber tone he tells me I should know this:
The lesion in my throat,
according to this note,
is malignant says the radiologist.

What have I experienced to this time?
Sometimes its painful in the neck,
the cancer's more than just a fleck
so treatment now should be foremost, yes prime.
I'm told the times ahead are rough
and my resolve must be enough
to get me through the doctor's treatment design.

Only God can give the strength
that I think I'll need at length
to navigate the times ahead
to find some peace in place of dread.

A Life Put On Hold

The news was bad but no surprise.
I have a cancer in my throat
which starting now I must devote
all energies to neutralize.

Plans I had for getting out:
hiking, travel, seeing sights
of scenic views and starry nights
and picking the less traveled route.

But then it all came tumbling down
as doctor after doctor confirmed
and diagnosis was again affirmed
that cancer was keeping me in town.

For it's quite a shock to get the word
that all your plans for months must end
as you fight this foe - your body mend.
Life for now will be deferred.

Proton therapy awaits,
as does chemo through the veins.
For now the body strains with pains
as treatments fill the coming dates.

To machines I now get tethered
which pump me up with chemo slurry
as days and weeks now all go blurry
in hopes their side-effects are weathered.

Added to this treatment plan
is radiation to burn it out
in a seemingly never ending bout
to get a cancer-free PT scan.

If all goes well and treatment prevails
seven weeks will be the course
it takes to bring a full divorce
and clear me of this cancer's ails.

So plans I had for setting out
to see more of the countryside
are now on hold, brushed aside
as healing's all I think about.

But remission's not the only end
that this destination knows.
It could be somehow fate bestows
a call I'd rather not attend.

So till that time the cancer's gone,
I'll know the fear that comes with dread.
For while the sword hangs 'or my head
I'll still have hope to draw upon.

A Cancer Perspective

I used to have nice shoulders, at least for a guy my size.
Each workout in the gym added to this prize.
But cancer has a way to rob you of your pride.
It will turn you inside out and take you for a ride.

The shoulders I once had are but a memory
for cancer sucks you dry, as one can clearly see.
But cancer came up short as I am breathing still
and if it should return I know the drill.

I will fight it tooth and nail
and God willing, I will prevail.

Walking Against The Wind

I'm trying hard to stay upbeat.
With news I've gotten that's no mean feat.
The cancer I had has gone away,
Another is back as of today.

Radiation and chemo too,
did all the things that they can do.
But cancer hides in unseen cells
and tells a tale that no one tells.

So this time we cut it out.
But twice burnt still leaves a doubt,
even though I'm on the mend
I'm forever walking against the wind.

Haiku

High-Key Haiku

Photograph high-key.
Lots of light in open shutter.
Notable object.

My Morning Walk

Morning sunlight shines
Crusty snow throws sparkles wide
Like mini prisms

Light came great distance
Countless sparkles just for me
On this brisk, cold day.

Limericks

Subtlety

Subtlety is a lost art,
something like a silent fart.
You know it's there,
but not from where,
and a message it will impart.

Retirement

A man's in a new world every day,
it does a wife little good to say
"I told you before,
but you just ignore.
So go on outside and play."

Marriage

Typically a husband and a wife
have seen their share of strife.
Instead of bugging
they should be hugging
it's key to a happier life.

Honey

I live in a challenging life,
with changes I should make being rife.
When it comes to money,
it flows like honey,
too slowly to ward off my strife.

What School?

Pull any student from the pool,
be they smart or be they a fool.
For students who yearn
their lessons to learn
matter much more than the school.

A Poet Named Thomas

A poet named Thomas I have read,
Yes Dylan is stuck within my head.
The things he said
were over my head
so I'll stick with Dr. Seuss instead.

Fire at Notre Dame

Mighty was Notre Dame,
gutted it was by the flame.
The steeple it fell,
we all fear as well
it will never again be the same.

Death of a Programmer

He was the best programmer in the town,
People knew him for miles around.
But he was old school,
Used cards like a fool,
So we buried him nine edge face down.

Limericks on Cancer

Losing Weight The Hard Way

I lost twenty-five pounds really fast.
It's a weight loss that will probably last.
To lose weight an answer
is to develop a cancer
to get rid of those pounds you've amassed.

Throat Cancer

Doctor said I had a choice,
it's to die or lose my voice.
My tongue he took,
My world it shook,
But I'm alive so now I rejoice.

Humor

Humor in the Garden of Eden

The Creation of Eve

Theologians everywhere
ask a question with great care:
When God created Eve
to whom Adam would cleave,
was the rib a prime or a spare?

An Unexpected Visitor

When Adam found Eve in the garden,
he said " Darling, I beg your pardon",
but is that your snake,
there by the lake,
or is my mother-in-law visiting again?

Expulsion From the Garden.

Adam I hear was a bore,
thought tending the garden was a chore.
So the apple he ate,
did not once hesitate,
so God showed him to the garden door.

Observing Mr. Bison

I see him from inside my car
I will see him from afar.
I'll not open up the gate.
I will not tempt my future fate.

Sitting here is close enough,
he looks mad and very tough.
He may not like green eggs and ham
so now moving on I am.

To Correct An Expression
(Pet Peeve)

It is incorrect to say
"I could care less"
it is correct to say
"I couldn't care less".

For "I could care less"
means you care some
while "I couldn't care less"
means that your care is none.

To The Reader:

Godspeed / Fare-thee-well

I wish you well upon your way
with many miles yet to go.
May they be safe for you this day,
come sun or rain or blowing snow.

The sun shine warm upon your path
with gentle breeze against your back.
May your way steer clear of wrath
with peace and joy to line your track.

So as you turn and bid adieu
my best wishes go with you.

About the author David Crowell is a retired Information Technology professional whose career was spent in the petroleum industry. He was engaging his hobbies of photography, travel, camping and hiking until cancer forced a lifestyle change, which he is now negotiating. He was also an active disaster relief volunteer through the Southern Baptist Convention.

Made in the USA
Coppell, TX
31 March 2022